D0948509

Law Enforcement

Bicycle Patrol Officers

by Michael Green

Consultant:
Officer Sandra Brown
Palo Alto Police Department
Palo Alto, California

RiverFront Books

an imprint of Franklin Watts
A Division of Grolier Publishing
New York   London   Hong Kong   Sydney
Danbury, Connecticut

RiverFront Books
http://publishing.grolier.com
Printed in the United States of America.
Published simultaneously in Canada.

Library of Congress Cataloging-in-Publication Data
Green, Michael, 1952–
    Bicycle patrol officers/by Michael Green.
    p. cm.—(Law enforcement)
    Summary: An introduction to the law enforcement officers known as
bicycle patrol officers, including their history, functions, responsibilities,
training, equipment, and the criminals they target.
    ISBN 0-7368-0186-3
    1. Bicycle police—United States—Juvenile literature. [1. Bicycle police.
2. Occupations.] I. Title. II. Series: Green, Michael, 1952– Law enforcement.
HV8019.G75 1999
363.2'32—dc21
                                                                98-46143
                                                                    CIP
                                                                     AC

Editorial Credits

Connie R. Colwell, editor; Timothy Halldin, cover designer; Kimberly Danger
    and Sheri Gosewisch, photo researchers

Photo Credits

Barbara J. Coxe, 6, 32
Diane Meyer, 8
Frances M. Roberts, 29, 39
Kirkendall/Spring, 17
Leslie O'Shaughnessy, cover, 18, 22, 24, 26, 34, 36, 40-41
Michael Green, 4, 12, 14, 21, 47
Transparencies, Inc./J.E. Glenn, 31
Visuals Unlimited, 11

Table of Contents

Chapter 1

Bicycle Patrol Officers

Bicycle patrol officers are police officers who patrol on bicycles. They have many of the same duties as other patrol officers. They help keep cities and towns safe. They help protect lives and property. They also help prevent crime. But these officers patrol on bicycles instead of in cars or on foot.

Patrolling on Bicycles

Patrolling on bicycles is not expensive. A police motorcycle costs about $10,000. A police patrol car costs about $25,000. But a police patrol bicycle costs less than $2,000. Cars and motorcycles use fuel to run. This also costs

Bicycle patrol officers patrol on bicycles.

Bicycles allow officers to patrol on sidewalks.

money. Cars and motorcycles cost more to repair than bicycles. One patrol car costs more than 10 times as much as one police patrol bicycle.

Bicycles are good for patrolling many areas. They allow officers to ride in and out of buildings. They allow officers to ride up and over stairs. Bicycle patrol officers can chase suspects in small areas such as between parked vehicles.

These officers can ride on sidewalks. They can go the wrong way on one-way streets. Officers in cars or motorcycles cannot do these things.

Bicycles are a quiet way to patrol. Bicycle patrol officers sometimes can sneak up on people who might be involved in crimes. Police cars and motorcycles are large and noisy. Officers who patrol by car or motorcycle cannot sneak up on these people.

In the Community

Bicycle patrol officers often get to know people in their communities. Many people are interested in bicycle patrol officers. These people can talk with the officers about their police work. Officers in police cars do not get as many chances to stop and talk with people in their communities.

Many bicycle patrol officers get to know people who live in neighborhoods where they patrol. These officers learn who lives in each neighborhood. This helps the officers spot strangers in the neighborhoods.

Chapter 2

History of Bicycle Patrol Officers

In the early 1800s, police officers in the United States and Canada patrolled on foot or horseback. These patrol methods had serious limits.

Many police officers patrolled on foot. But officers on foot could not go very fast or far. They could only patrol small areas.

Other patrol officers rode horses. These mounted patrol officers could go fast enough to catch suspects. But the horses in mounted units needed a great deal of care. The horses sometimes got sick. They needed food and

Horses in mounted patrol units need a great deal of care.

water. They also needed large places to stay. Many police departments wanted a faster and easier way to patrol.

The Bicycle Patrol

At the end of the 1800s, New York was the largest city in the United States. More than 1.5 million people lived there. People in New York traveled by horses or horse-drawn carriages. These wagons are used to carry people. Horses and carriages crowded the city's streets.

Some people drove their horse-drawn carriages too fast. Many people in New York were hit by speeding carriages. Some of them even died.

In 1895, Theodore Roosevelt was in charge of the New York Police Department (NYPD). Roosevelt wanted to control the city's traffic problems. He formed a bicycle patrol unit to help solve the city's traffic problems.

Officers on bicycles traveled faster and farther than officers on foot. A police officer on foot could not catch a speeding horse-drawn carriage. But a police officer on a bicycle might

At the end of the 1800s, New York was the largest city in the United States.

be able to catch the carriage. A police officer on foot could not stop a person committing a crime many streets away. But an officer on a bicycle could travel much faster. The officer then could try to stop the person.

Many police departments in other cities also formed bicycle patrol units. These units helped control traffic problems throughout the United States and Canada.

Motor Patrols

In the early 1900s, cars began to replace horse-drawn carriages. Police officers on bicycles could not travel as fast as speeding cars. In 1911, the NYPD formed a motorcycle unit. Motorcycles could travel as fast as cars.

In 1919, the NYPD formed a car patrol unit. The NYPD began to replace its bicycles with cars. Police departments throughout the United States and Canada also formed car patrol units. Car and motorcycle patrol units replaced bicycle patrol units throughout the United States and Canada.

Police officers on bicycles could not travel as fast as speeding cars.

Chapter 3

Modern Bicycle Patrol Officers

In the 1980s, some police departments needed a better way to patrol crowded city streets. They needed to move quickly through small spaces and traffic jams. Police departments began forming bicycle patrol units again.

Beach Patrol

Before the 1980s, some police departments in California used bicycles to patrol beaches. Cars and motorcycles are too large and noisy to patrol beaches effectively. Bicycles are small and quiet. They are easy to control on sandy beaches.

Some police departments in California used bicycles to patrol beaches during the summer.

Some police departments in California use bicycles to patrol beaches.

But most of these police departments did not use bicycles for beach patrol all year. Bicycles can be difficult to ride in rainy or cold weather. These departments still used cars and motorcycles for most of their patrol work.

Traffic Problems

In 1987, the downtown area of Seattle, Washington, was being rebuilt. Construction work made it difficult for people to drive on the downtown streets. The construction caused many traffic problems.

The construction also caused problems for the Seattle Police Department (SPD). Police cars got stuck in the traffic. They could not patrol the downtown area quickly. The crime rate in downtown Seattle went up.

Jim Deschane was the police captain in charge of Seattle's downtown area. Deschane wanted better ways to patrol the downtown area. He asked his officers for ideas. Some officers suggested patrolling with motor scooters or small, off-road motorcycles. But

Crowded downtown Seattle streets are difficult to patrol by car.

Bicycles can be used to patrol places other patrol vehicles cannot.

motor vehicles could not patrol on sidewalks or in parks. Deschane had to find a different way to patrol Seattle's streets.

A New Solution

Police officers Paul Grady and Mike Miller worked for Deschane. Grady and Miller had patrolled the downtown area in police cars. They also had patrolled on foot. They knew these ways of patrolling could be difficult. Grady and Miller rode bicycles in their free time. They suggested that the downtown officers use bicycles to patrol.

Deschane told the SPD chief about Grady and Miller's idea. The chief let Grady and Miller try to patrol on bicycles.

The Seattle Bicycle Patrol

On July 10, 1987, Grady and Miller began to patrol the streets of downtown Seattle by bicycle. They arrested three drug dealers in the first 30 minutes of their patrol. Grady and Miller arrested hundreds of suspects in the next month. They made four times as many arrests as officers in police cars.

The SPD expanded its bicycle patrol unit. The SPD assigned about 30 more officers to the bicycle patrol. It also assigned bicycle officers to patrol other areas of Seattle. Today, the SPD has more than 60 bicycle patrol officers. The SPD bicycle patrol unit helps control crime throughout Seattle.

More Bicycle Patrol Units

Many people became interested in the SPD bicycle patrol. Newspapers, TV stations, and radio stations reported on the bicycle patrol officers. Other police departments also became interested in the SPD bicycle patrol. They wanted to know how to start their own bicycle patrol units.

Today, there are more than 1,300 U.S. and Canadian police departments with bicycle patrol units. Many military, park, school, and security guard forces also use bicycles to patrol. These bicycle patrol units help patrol communities in the United States and Canada.

Today, many police departments use bicycles to patrol.

Chapter 4

Training

Police officers need special training to become bicycle patrol officers. They must know how to ride police bicycles. They must know how to fix their bicycles. Bicycle patrol officers also must be in good physical shape.

Bicycle Patrol Unit Training

The first Seattle Police Department (SPD) bicycle patrol officers were not trained to patrol on bicycles. The officers did not know the best ways to ride their bicycles in busy traffic. Bicycle shop owners and mountain bike racers helped the officers learn the necessary skills. These people taught the officers how to ride safely. They also taught them how to repair their bicycles.

Bicycle patrol officers must know how to fix their bicycles.

In late 1987, the SPD formed a training program for its bicycle patrol officers. Today, many other police departments have similar bicycle training programs.

The officers study many things in the training programs. Officers study the parts of police bicycles. They learn how to repair their bicycles. They learn how to ride bicycles on all types of terrain. They practice riding on off-road trails. They practice riding up and down stairs. They learn to ride on crowded city streets.

Physical Condition

Bicycle patrol officers must be in good physical condition. They often ride their bicycles all day. Sometimes they need to ride very fast or for a long time without stopping.

Most officers have to pass a physical test before they can join a bicycle patrol unit. Doctors measure the officers' leg strength, body fat, and heart rate. These measurements show whether the officers are healthy and in good condition.

Bicycle patrol officers have training programs to help them learn to ride their bicycles.

Chapter 5

Bicycles and Uniforms

Bicycle patrol officers need special bicycles and uniforms. These officers use strong bicycles called mountain bikes to patrol. Officers can ride mountain bikes on all types of terrain. Bicycle patrol officers wear special uniforms. These uniforms allow the officers to stay comfortable while they are riding their mountain bikes.

Mountain Bikes

Mountain bikes are sturdy enough to handle many types of terrain and weather. Some cities have many hills. Others have many off-road trails. Some cities have a great deal of rain.

Bicycle patrol officers use mountain bikes to patrol.

Mountain bikes can handle this various land and weather.

Most mountain bikes are lightweight and sturdy. Many are made out of steel or aluminum. Steel and aluminum are strong, lightweight metals. These metals make the mountain bikes lighter and easier to handle. Most mountain bikes weigh from 26 to 30 pounds (12 to 14 kilograms).

Mountain bikes have tires to help them grip the ground. These tires are made of thick rubber. The rubber tires keep the bikes from slipping on ice or gravel. Mountain bike tires also have tread. These bumps and deep grooves help the tires grip slippery ground.

Most mountain bikes have gear shifters on their handlebars. Officers shift gears when they need to ride on different types of land. Some gears make it easier for officers to pedal uphill. Others help the officers pedal on flat land. Most police mountain bikes have 18 gears.

Mountain bike tires have tread to help them grip
the ground.

Uniforms

The first SPD bicycle patrol officers wore the
same uniforms as other officers. The bicycle
patrol officers wore short-sleeved shirts and
long pants. They wore heavy black leather
shoes and thick leather belts. But the officers
were hot and uncomfortable in these uniforms.

They needed uniforms that kept them cool while they rode their bicycles. They also needed uniforms that allowed their legs to move freely during pedaling.

Today, bicycle patrol officers wear cotton bicycle shorts in warm weather. Cotton is a soft cloth that helps officers keep cool. Cotton shorts also make it easy for officers to pedal. The officers wear long pants in cooler weather. The pants also are made of cotton.

Many bicycle patrol officers wear fingerless gloves. These special gloves cover the officers' hands. But they do not cover the officers' fingers. These gloves keep the officers' hands warm in cold weather. They keep officers' fingers free for shifting gears. The gloves also help protect officers' hands if the officers fall off their bikes.

Bicycle patrol officers wear special uniforms to keep them comfortable while riding their bikes.

Chapter 6

Equipment and Safety

Bicycle patrol officers' jobs can be risky. The officers need protection from accidents and criminal suspects. They have special gear and rules to help keep them safe.

Bicycle Safety

Police bicycles need special safety equipment. Most police bicycles have lights and reflectors. Some have fenders. This equipment helps keep officers safe when they ride their bicycles.

Lights and reflectors are important safety features on police bicycles. Most police bicycles have lights and reflectors on the front and rear. Some bicycles also have reflectors on

Police bicycles have lights on their handlebars to help the officers see where they are going.

their wheels. Lights help officers see where they are going. Reflectors reflect light from motor vehicles' headlights back to the motorists. Reflectors and lights help motorists see the officers on mountain bikes.

Bicycle patrol officers must sometimes ride in the rain. Their bicycles have fenders. These metal or plastic covers are attached to the front and rear wheels of bicycles. Fenders keep water from splashing the officers.

Weapon Safety

Bicycle patrol officers carry guns. Most carry semiautomatic pistols. Officers squeeze triggers to shoot these pistols. The pistols then load a bullet for the next shot. These pistols help officers protect themselves and others. Officers only use their pistols when necessary.

The officers also carry holsters and bullets. Holsters hold pistols until officers need to use them. The holsters attach to the officers' belts. Most semiautomatic pistols hold from 15 to

Holsters hold pistols until the officers need to use them.

17 bullets. Officers carry extra bullets in small pouches that hang from their belts.

The officers have a weapon rule to help keep them safe. The officers may not fire their pistols while they are riding their bicycles. They must stop and get off their bicycles first. This helps officers control their pistols. Then, the officers can fire their pistols. This rule helps prevent pistol accidents.

Most officers wear armored vests under their shirts. These vests help protect the officers from bullets. The vests are made of soft material. This material helps keep officers comfortable.

Other Safety Equipment

All bicycle patrol officers wear safety helmets. Helmets help protect the officers' heads from falls and other accidents. The word "POLICE" is on both sides of most bicycle officers' helmets. This helps people recognize bicycle patrol officers as police officers.

Bicycle patrol officers must get off their bicycles before they can fire their pistols.

Some bicycle patrol officers wear special glasses. These glasses protect officers' eyes from sun and other dangers. The sun can shine in officers' eyes and make it hard to see. Dust and bugs also can get caught in their eyes. Small rocks kicked up by passing vehicles can injure officers' eyes. Glasses protect the officers' eyes from all these dangers.

Some officers use whistles or bells. Officers wear whistles on ropes or strings around their necks. Officers put warning bells on their bikes. The whistles and bells tell people that bicyclists are nearby.

Some officers carry pepper spray. Pepper spray is an irritant. Irritants bother the parts of the body that they touch. Some suspects can become out of control and dangerous. Officers may spray pepper spray into these suspects' eyes. The pepper spray can make the suspects' eyes water and hurt. The spray also can make it more difficult for the suspects to breathe. Then, the officers can control the suspects and calm them down.

Bicycle patrol officers keep communities safe
for many people.

Safe Communities

Bicycle patrol officers are an important part of
many police departments. They patrol crowded
areas. They help control crime and enforce laws.

Bicycle patrol officers protect many people
every day. They work hard to keep communities
safe for people throughout the United States
and Canada.

Police Mountain Bike

Seat

Reflector

Tread

Police Label

Gear
Shifters

Tire

Reflector

Words to Know

aluminum (uh-LOO-mi-nuhm)—a lightweight, silver-colored metal

fender (FEN-dur)—a metal or plastic cover over the wheel of a bicycle that protects the wheel against damage and reduces splashing

gear shifters (GIHR SHIFT-urz)—levers on a bicycle that allow officers to change the movement of a bicycle; some gears help officers ride up or down hills.

holster (HOHL-stur)—a holder for a gun

irritant (IHR-uh-tuhnt)—something that bothers certain parts of the body

mountain bike (MOUN-tuhn BIKE)—a bicycle with knobby tires that is strong enough to be used on rough or hilly ground

patrol (puh-TROHL)—to walk or travel around an area to protect it or to keep watch

semiautomatic (sem-ee-aw-tuh-MAT-ik)—partly operated by hand and partly operated by itself; bicycle patrol officers carry semiautomatic pistols.

suspect (SUHS-pekt)—someone officers think might be responsible for a crime

terrain (tuh-RAYN)—the surface of the land; mountain bikes travel easily over rough terrain.

tread (TRED)—deep grooves and ridges on a bicycle tire that help prevent slipping

To Learn More

Cohen, Paul and Shari Cohen. *Careers in Law Enforcement and Security*. New York: Rosen Publishing Group, 1995.

Green, Michael. *Motorcycle Police*. Law Enforcement. Mankato, Minn.: RiverFront Books, 1999.

Green, Michael. *Mounted Police*. Law Enforcement. Mankato, Minn.: RiverFront Books, 1998.

Useful Addresses

The International Police Mountain Bike Association
1612 K Street NW
Suite 401
Washington, D.C. 20006

Law Enforcement Bicycle Association
823 Snipe Ireland Road
Richmond, VT 05477-9604

New York City Police Department
Public Affairs Office
One Police Plaza
New York, NY 10038

Royal Canadian Mounted Police
Box 8885
Ottawa, ON K1G 3M8
Canada

Internet Sites

Canadian Police Agency
http://police.sas.ab.ca/local/zcanada.html

Law Enforcement Bicycle Association
http://www.leba.org

New York City Police Department
http://www.ci.nyc.ny.us/html/nypd

Royal Canadian Mounted Police
http://www.rcmp-grc.gc.ca/html/rcmp2.htm

Seattle Police Home Page
http://www.ci.seattle.wa.us/spd/spdpan.htm

Index